MINI MESSAGES FROM GOD

Linda K. Henderson

BK
ROYSTON
Publishing

BK Royston Publishing
P. O. Box 4321
Jeffersonville, IN 47131
http://www.bkroystonpublishing.com
bkroystonpublishing@gmail.com

Cover Design: Elite Book Covers

ISBN-13: 978-1-959543-06-0

Printed in the United States of America

Dedication

Mini Messages is written for and dedicated to any child of God who wishes to know our Creator more intimately. It is for anyone who wonders what is ahead and the choices that are available to them.

Acknowledgements

I give all the glory to God for providing me with the inspiration, input, and introduction to the material that has become Mini Messages from God. To my husband who encouraged me, supported me, and pushed me to go forward. To my oldest daughter Taryn, who sent a microphone to dictate my words which made my job easier. To my middle daughter Astarre' who is already arranging book signings and readings. To my youngest daughter Ebone', the photographer, that provided a photo shoot for my Bio Picture.

I also would like to acknowledge my former Pastors, Peter and Marsha Williams, without whom I would not be who I am in Christ today. My present Pastor, Elder Gregory Williams, First Lady, Debbie Williams and my Rocky Ford Church family that continues to teach and inspire me. I would like to thank my best friend, Evangelist Karen Burton, to my dear friends Helen Clark and Sister Barbara Gary who encouraged me immensely and so many others, you know who you are.

Thank you and I love you all.

Table Of Contents

Dedication   iii

Acknowledgements   v

Introduction   vii

Bless The Lord   1

Wait For Him   5

His Power   9

An Appointed Time   13

His Grace   17

Cast Your Cares   21

Imagine   25

Oh That Men   29

We Are Rich   33

It's Testimony Time   37

Good Steward   41

At the Table   45

Muscle Memory   49

Employment To Deployment   53

Rare Pearls   57

What Ails You?   61

Judgment   65

What Would We Do?   69

What Is Your Motive?   73

Hiding Places   77

Write the Vision   81

Friends   85

Change   89

Superpowers   93

Say It Loud   97

Practice Prayer   101

Reclaim Your Day   105

Identity Crisis   109

SOS   113

Before You Speak — Think   117

Be Thankful   121

FOMO   125

Reverent Demands   129

Think on These Things   133

It Takes a Village   137

Contrasts   141

Courageous   145

Introduction

Mini Messages from God came from a desire to have my messages seen and read by a multitude of people. Not just a Christian audience, but people who are curious and like me, did not understand the word of God. Mini Messages is insightful and simplistic enough that even a child can understand. It is written that we might inspire people young and old to connect with God's vision.

Bless the Lord

Psalm 103:1–5

"Bless the Lord, O my soul; And all that is within me, bless His holy name! Bless the Lord, O my soul, And forget not all His benefits: Who forgives all your iniquities, Who heals all your diseases, Who redeems your life from destruction, Who crowns you with lovingkindness and tender mercies, Who satisfies your mouth with good things, So that your youth is renewed like the eagle's." (NKJV)

He forgives all our iniquities, so do not think of the Lord as waiting and watching for you to do something wrong. Thinking that He might whack you over the head every time you make the wrong move, think the wrong thought, say the wrong thing. God is waiting for us to do something right. As you strive to serve Him, bless the Lord for the many benefits that He has bestowed upon you. He's not holding them against us. When our children stumble and fall, we encourage them to get up, to try it again, and assure them that they can do it.

He heals all our diseases. Name above all names, Jesus Christ is the big C — not cancer, not coronavirus — but Christ is the big C. Thank Him for pulling our lives from destruction and keeping you away from harmful thoughts and earthly things. Thank Him for loving kindness and tender mercies. Even amid our mistakes, He looks at us as newborn babes learning to crawl and then to walk and then to pray and then to believe.

Jesus loves us. He gives us good things to satisfy our mouth that our youth be renewed as the eagle's. He gives us His word to speak healing, to speak blessings and to bestow hope in others' lives. Not only spiritual things, but also good things to eat for our health and beneficial for our lives, our youthful zest and zeal for Him is restored. Whether it is my fault or someone else's fault, the attempt of the enemy to kill, steal and destroy everything in our lives is real. Remember His benefits and bless Him with our lives.

Prayer: Thank You, Lord, for renewing my youth as the eagle's for Your benefits and Your love. I pray for continued growth and understanding; keep me close and living in Your will. In Jesus' name. Amen.

Your Reflections

How Can You Apply This Message to Your Life?

_____
_____
_____
_____
_____
_____
_____
_____
_____
_____
_____
_____
_____
_____
_____
_____
_____
_____
_____
_____
_____
_____
_____
_____
_____

Your Reflections

How Can You Apply This Message to Your Life?

_____
_____
_____
_____
_____
_____
_____
_____
_____
_____
_____
_____
_____
_____
_____
_____
_____
_____
_____
_____
_____
_____
_____
_____
_____

Wait for Him

Isaiah 40:31

But they that wait upon the Lord shall renew their strength; they shall mount up with wings as eagles; they shall run, and not be weary; and they shall walk, and not faint. (KJV)

We have been informed that we must wait on the Lord for answers to prayers, to be blessed, to move up another level. It happens in all areas of our lives — to be promoted at work, to be approved by others or recognized at all. All the above is true; however, as we wait as a waitress or a waiter, we serve the Lord with our time, our talents and our gifts. The waiting period seems shorter, not as excruciating, as we serve Him and others. A heart has time to heal, our minds clear and our wait time has restored our bodies; we can mount up on wings as eagles, run and not get weary, walk and not faint.

Once a year, eagles go up as high as they can and sit before the sun and pluck their feathers one by one and wait for their feathers to grow back. They are vulnerable, but they wait for new feathers to appear, restored when the wait is over, they are better than ever. The old feathers would give them away as they hunted for prey; their strength is renewed, so are we as we wait and pray. Daily the eagles, one by one, steam their feathers, sharpening their skills so they are ready for the day. We have to get before the Son and do the same.

Prayer: Thank You, Father, for my youth and strength being renewed. Thank You that Your Word gives me hope and encouragement. I pray that You continue to give me the courage to wait on whatever You have in store for me. In Jesus' name. Amen.

Your Reflections

How Can You Apply This Message to Your Life?

_____

_____

_____

_____

_____

_____

_____

_____

_____

_____

_____

_____

_____

_____

_____

_____

_____

_____

_____

_____

_____

_____

_____

_____

_____

Your Reflections

How Can You Apply This Message to Your Life?

_____
_____
_____
_____
_____
_____
_____
_____
_____
_____
_____
_____
_____
_____
_____
_____
_____
_____
_____
_____
_____
_____
_____
_____

His Power

Ecclesiastes 4:12

And if one prevail against him, two shall withstand him; and a threefold cord is not quickly broken. (KJV)

We all know that there is power in numbers, and this scripture is saying that if there are two of you, there's help in a dangerous situation. If there are three, there is hope. It is threefold when you think about Jesus and how good He is and about all He has done for us. We know that God sent Him to show His love, to reconnect, to reconcile us back to Him and to pave the way to give us salvation. To be honest, we don't think about the third person that was sent to us individually and is the resolution to what we all needed. I was speaking with a friend about the Holy Ghost and agreed that people are afraid of or apprehensive about Him being called the Holy Ghost and prefer to say Holy Spirit. However, when you have a relationship with the precious spirit of God when He has comforted you in times of need, when He has rebuked you, and kept you safe from harm, then you don't fear one name over the other; you are just aware that the three are one: Father, Son and Holy Ghost. They are all working on our behalf; all three were there in the beginning and as the three works in unison we have the victory and are successful. We are winners and the power that is all three is ours as well. The spirit of God is our companion and is also known as the paraclete, our advocate, our counselor, our helper.

Prayer: Thank You, Father, that in the name of Jesus we pray by Your spirit to You. We don't know what to pray without the Holy Spirit. Thank You for Your Son and spirit. I pray that through Your word more will come to the knowledge of You. That they will know Your Spirit and employ His guidance and presence in their everyday life. Help us to understand the help that Jesus promised is here inside of us. In Jesus' name I pray. Amen.

Your Reflections

How Can You Apply This Message to Your Life?

_____

_____

_____

_____

_____

_____

_____

_____

_____

_____

_____

_____

_____

_____

_____

_____

_____

_____

_____

_____

_____

_____

_____

_____

_____

Your Reflections

How Can You Apply This Message to Your Life?

_____

_____

_____

_____

_____

_____

_____

_____

_____

_____

_____

_____

_____

_____

_____

_____

_____

_____

_____

_____

_____

_____

_____

_____

An Appointed Time

Genesis 1:14–19

And God said, "Let there be lights in the vault of the sky to separate the day from the night, and let them serve as signs to mark sacred times, and days and years, and let them be lights in the vault of the sky to give light on the earth." And it was so. God made two great lights — the greater light to govern the day and the lesser light to govern the night. He also made the stars. God set them in the vault of the sky to give light on the earth, to govern the day and the night, and to separate light from darkness. And God saw that it was good. And there was evening, and there was morning — the fourth day. (NIV)

On the fourth day of creation, God divided day and night with sun, moon and stars; also the division of days, years and seasons were made. God established appointed times for seasons as He also has appointed times for us. The word states that He knew us before we were planted in our mother's wombs and had a plan and a purpose for us. The enemy, being an impersonator of God, had one as well.

God's plan supersedes the enemy's plan. The word says that He would not have us ignorant of his devices. God has an appointed time for things in our lives, and the enemy's job is to stop it. We are well equipped with His assistance to accomplish His plan, not without Him, but with Him every step of the way.

Remember that God's way for us is not to keep us from fun in this life, but to keep us from harm. Smoking, drinking and other worldly things will not keep us from our purpose, but will make our life harder. He has rules and regulations to keep you safe. There are road rules that tell you the speed limit is 35mph, but we will go 50 or 75 or more. The rules or there for safety, so when we wreck the car or wreck our lives not discerning God's purpose, sometimes we miss an appointed time.

God is not waiting for us to fail; He is encouraging us to get up and try again. He is not waiting to overtake you and make you feel ashamed, but to empower you to encourage you and to carry you every step of the way, if need be. God is watching you not for condemnation but for your confirmation. If we need more time, we can ask.

Prayer: Thank You, Father, for Your appointed times; thank You that You have it all planned out for us. I pray for wisdom and insight to accomplish Your will. Thanks for the victory. All the glory belongs to You. In Jesus' name. Amen.

Your Reflections

How Can You Apply This Message to Your Life?

_____

_____

_____

_____

_____

_____

_____

_____

_____

_____

_____

_____

_____

_____

_____

_____

_____

_____

_____

_____

_____

_____

His Grace

Romans 6:1

Shall we continue in sin, that grace may abound?
(KJV)

Paul replies to his own question, "God forbid." Grace is the unmerited favor of God. A gift, finally, we can't earn and we can't lose. With this favor, we received the eradication of guilt, no more condemnation, no more shame. With repentance and prayer, we can continue with God's purpose and plan for our lives.

We are under grace — a wonderful, marvelous gift from God. Everything is lawful for us but not profitable. If we think eating meat will harm others, because to them it's sin, just say "no." If a friend has a drug or drinking addiction, abstain yourself for their benefit. Eventually, that brother or sister will grow in the grace that we have all received and understand.

It's not the world's way, but what the Word says that keeps us walking in grace not away from it. There is no more sacrificing or any other atonement for sin. You cannot buy your way in or go around. Receive grace and Jesus' sacrifice as an appropriate and redeeming action for us through love.

Prayer: Father God, thank You for Your unmerited favor in Jesus Christ. Thank You that You allowed us to grow in it, understanding that grace is not a free pass to do as we please but an opportunity to do Your will. Thanks for the freedom to choose life and not death in every area of our lives. In Jesus' name. Amen.

Your Reflections

How Can You Apply This Message to Your Life?

_____

_____

_____

_____

_____

_____

_____

_____

_____

_____

_____

_____

_____

_____

_____

_____

_____

_____

_____

_____

_____

_____

_____

_____

_____

Your Reflections

How Can You Apply This Message to Your Life?

_____
_____
_____
_____
_____
_____
_____
_____
_____
_____
_____
_____
_____
_____
_____
_____
_____
_____
_____
_____
_____
_____
_____
_____
_____
_____

Cast Your Cares

1 Peter 5:7

[Cast] all your care upon Him, for He cares for you. (NKJV)

Lord, I don't know how, I don't know when, but You do. I can't imagine or even understand, but You do. So, help me Lord to hold fast to my profession and my confession of faith in You. Keep me in peace and let me rest in You. I cast my cares on You, for You care for me.

This is my favorite conversation with the Lord, something that He has heard from me repeatedly, my cry out to Him, "You know Lord, I don't understand." This cry is a staple in my relationship with my Father in heaven. It is an awesome promise that I am always cared for, that we should consider in times of distress. I come and make my request known to You. We do not have to be worried or anxious about our situations and circumstances, we go to our Father first, not our friends or family, Facebook, or self-help book. We go to our God in prayer.

Do not hold on to your problem, situation and circumstance for too long. Like a hot potato, toss it off to God. He knows the way out; He has the solution and will help you out. Cast your cares on Him, for He cares for you. Knowing when to use and what to use in your spiritual toolkit is masterful and cannot be taken away. Become adept at applying them for maximum benefit.

Prayer: Thank You, Lord, for having everything in Your toolkit to fix or care for me; thank You for the peace that passes understanding. Thank You that You know the beginning and the end that You are the Alpha and the Omega. Thank You that I can depend on You and have faith in You to make Your promises come to pass in my life. In Jesus' name. Amen.

Your Reflections

How Can You Apply This Message to Your Life?

_____

_____

_____

_____

_____

_____

_____

_____

_____

_____

_____

_____

_____

_____

_____

_____

_____

_____

_____

_____

_____

_____

_____

Your Reflections

How Can You Apply This Message to Your Life?

_____
_____
_____
_____
_____
_____
_____
_____
_____
_____
_____
_____
_____
_____
_____
_____
_____
_____
_____
_____
_____
_____
_____
_____
_____

Imagine

Genesis 1:26–27

Then God said, "Let us make mankind in our image, in our likeness...." So God created mankind in his own image, in the image of God he created them.... (NKJV)

Imagine foolish people on the world stage, actors on the religious and political theater, the big picture if you will. God looking down on all of this, imagine how it appears to Him. Hatred on all sides. Hunger in all spaces no matter how rich we are. Hidden dangers in all walks of life, nature polluted and ravaged, no crops grow in places and in others, pesticides ruined the land and our health. Imagine God taking it all in, looking at the world map, changing and rearranging, putting the puzzle pieces together, saving, encouraging and making a way of escape for us.

All this while we accept Jesus Christ as our savior, believing in our hearts and confessing with our mouths that Jesus is the Son of God, that he is our Lord. Imagine — individually we follow Christ, a lamp and a light. Find and follow His plan for us from the foundation, before we were planted in our mother's womb. Imagine collectively the church loving one another being part of the solution, not the problem.

Imagine changing your way of thinking, of loving, of laying down your life for a friend. So that when men look at your life, they glorify God so that people can see the contrast. Jesus wept; He cried over Jerusalem before He went in; He saw their future and His own; He knew what would happen. No, we're not in Jerusalem, but we can apply it to our lives today. He looks at us with the love of God on his face; we were created for Him for his enjoyment for his companionship and to show His love. No matter what the map looks like, God desires us. We don't have to imagine; the truth is in the Word. The truth is in our heart.

Prayer: Thank You, Lord, for desiring us. Knowing what You know, still Your desire is for us. Thank You for Your love; thank You for Your patience; thank You for forgiving us no matter what. The heart of the king is in Your hand. So we ask, Lord God, in the name of Jesus that You touch the kings of this world, the presidents of this world and the prime ministers of this world that reside on the map. Lord God, help us see the changes that You make in each one of us individually and collectively. We thank You that Your heart is toward us, that Your face shines upon us. Do with us what You please. In the name of Jesus. Amen.

Your Reflections

How Can You Apply This Message to Your Life?

_____
_____
_____
_____
_____
_____
_____
_____
_____
_____
_____
_____
_____
_____
_____
_____
_____
_____
_____
_____
_____
_____
_____
_____

Oh That Men

Psalm 107:8

Oh that men would praise the Lord for his goodness, and for his wonderful works to the children of men! (KJV)

We have wandered in the wilderness of our situations and circumstances far too long. Oh that men would praise the Lord for His goodness: He has delivered us from old ways, old houses, no houses, and from abusive houses. We have been brought out, the old ways of thinking and doing, our way, leaning to our own understanding. Jesus took on all that we had need of; He suffered and sacrificed so that we can stand where we are now. We can recognize what He has done for us. Will we praise Him for His goodness? Read the whole of Psalm 107 and see yourself, your situation. What has He bought you out of? How many times has He bought you out? He paid the price for you and me.

There are things we have heard, read, and talked about, but have never done in the Word of God. When we show love to one and not the other, then it negates the love we say we have. If that love is not toward everyone, is it God led or your head? (Head is dangerous; that is where the enemy plays).

Oh, that men would praise the Lord for his goodness. Praising the Lord and remembering his goodness keeps us grounded, keeps us from crashing and burning. Envy, jealousy and unforgiveness takes us down the path of unrighteousness. We are the righteousness of God in Christ Jesus; oh, that men would praise the Lord for his goodness.

Prayer: I thank You, Lord, for helping us to remember who You are. To remember what You have done for us. Thank You, Lord, for bringing us down the path of righteousness. I praise You for showing us Your will. Forgetting what You have sacrificed causes us to harbor bitterness and lose our way and we become ignorant of the devices of the enemy. I praise You for Your goodness. I praise You, Jesus, for Your wonderful works toward the children of men. Amen.

Your Reflections

How Can You Apply This Message to Your Life?

_____

_____

_____

_____

_____

_____

_____

_____

_____

_____

_____

_____

_____

_____

_____

_____

_____

_____

_____

_____

_____

_____

_____

_____

_____

_____

_____

Your Reflections

How Can You Apply This Message to Your Life?

_____

_____

_____

_____

_____

_____

_____

_____

_____

_____

_____

_____

_____

_____

_____

_____

_____

_____

_____

_____

_____

_____

_____

We Are Rich

Philippians 4:19

And my God shall supply all your need according to his riches and glory by Christ Jesus. (NKJV)

Money is not the only thing that makes us rich. In Christ Jesus we have spiritual provision; we are rich in grace, which is the unmerited favor of God. We are rich in mercy, goodness, wisdom and understanding. We are rich because the Word says if we ask anything in Jesus' name it will be given to us. We are rich in Christ Jesus — saved, sanctified, set apart unto him. We are rich in everything He took to the cross with Him, in restoration, deliverance, healing, health, success. We are rich because we have an advocate in Jesus.

It is not how much money we put in church, how many hours we work. It's part of our riches because of the promises concerning those things. If a man doesn't work, he doesn't eat. The Word has promises concerning tithes and offerings: be a cheerful giver and purpose in your own heart what you're going to give. These things are important; however, they're not the principal things. We are rich in talents and gifts to use to the glory of God. We all have our own. We are rich in the fruit of the spirit love, joy, peace, goodness, gentleness, kindness, faithfulness — we are rich in Christ Jesus.

We can love because He first loved us. Love covers a multitude of sin; if we say we love God and only some of our brothers and sisters, then we lie. It's easy to love those who love us and enable us sometimes, but the Word says He loved us first while we were still in sin. Jesus says, "who is my mother and my sister, the ones that believe as I believe." The love that we share in Christ Jesus, is for all.

Once again, we are rich because God has forgiven us and can help us to forgive others. We are rich because He sent His Son. We are rich even when we have frailties and lose our way; God's love is always present. He will make a way of escape for us. It is better to give than to receive. We are rich when we have something to give.

We are rich because we are permitted to come to church to do our part in the service. Singing and preparing the music, saying the prayers, reading scriptures, bringing the message. We may not feel worthy to do our job, but God has set us up for success with his Son Jesus Christ. Sometimes, like David, we must encourage ourselves.

Prayer: Thank You, Lord, for the richness You have afforded us. Thank You for encouraging us to remember our blessings and understanding the part we play in Your kingdom. Thank You for the gifts You have placed inside of us. Please continue to help us in our everyday life to do Your will. In Jesus' name. Amen.

Your Reflections

How Can You Apply This Message to Your Life?

_____

_____

_____

_____

_____

_____

_____

_____

_____

_____

_____

_____

_____

_____

_____

_____

_____

_____

_____

_____

_____

_____

_____

_____

_____

It's Testimony Time

John 8:17–18

"It is also written in your law that the testimony of two men is true. I am One who bears witness of Myself, and the Father who sent Me bears witness of Me."

At church during devotion, after we have said the prayer, after we have read a scripture and responsive reading, it would be time for testimony.

My mother —- I would talk to my mother on the phone almost every night and day. In one of these conversations, she told me about watching a TV ministry that she would send money to. The ministry she watched was quite controversial and seemed to attract unwanted attention. I asked her not to continue supporting this ministry, that all "those" people wanted was her money. She continued to do so, until I, striving to prove her wrong, started watching the program myself.

Myself — From that point on, I never said another word to my mother about her choice of programing and stopped insisting she not watch that show. I heard a word that grabbed me and changed my life. I would watch with her on the phone. The preacher was very charismatic and animated. God was his friend and I wanted to be His friend as well. It was several years before I learned about giving and why I should give. However, when I started giving, I never stopped. Thanks to my mom.

My daughter — While traveling to visit my daughters and grandchildren, my oldest daughter began to talk about her experience with tithing and offering. She informed me that it took a while before she thought she could afford to give. She gradually made the adjustment over time, and she would give ten percent. She said, "I knew you gave a lot" (that's subjective), but she didn't think she could. However, gradually she grew in wisdom and grace. In our conversation, she also said that she thought her tithing was the reason she got her first home. The gentleman that was looking at her paperwork said, "I see you are a tither." Thanks, Mom.

Moral — God can draw us in many ways: it is not always suddenly, immediately or expeditiously, but slow and steady. Leaving a legacy that can be passed on for generations.

Prayer: Thank You Lord that every day in every generation You make Yourself known in special ways. Thank You, that You can pass good and anointed blessings our way. Thank You for Your plan and purpose coming to fruition. In Jesus' name. Amen.

Your Reflections

How Can You Apply This Message to Your Life?

_____

_____

_____

_____

_____

_____

_____

_____

_____

_____

_____

_____

_____

_____

_____

_____

_____

_____

_____

_____

_____

_____

_____

_____

Good Steward

Luke 16:2

So he called him and said to him, "What is this I hear about you? Give an account of your stewardship, for you can no longer be steward." (NKJV)

Being a good steward is more than time, money, and material things. Sticking your head in the sand, ignoring slights, sleeping spiritual sleep, believing that if people like you, all is well. We must take the time to discern the spirit and carry our own weight. You have a partnership at work, at church, at home. We cannot just care for ourselves; we have to care for others and each other. What we think is not correct all the time, we can't just hear the Word we have to speak the Word and we must do the Word.

We must share responsibility, one not carrying all the load or taking all the load oneself, because you want it your way. A balance is needed: trust God, do not lean to your own understanding, bring your best to the table. We need to recognize the enemy; he does not like us. He wants to kill, steal, destroy and ruin everything associated with you.

People do not show love the same; some are givers, will give you the shirt off their back, will give you their last dollar. Others are supporters and will support you in all your endeavors even financially. Don't think your way is better: just say "thank you." Also, be aware of the dangers in believing you know best.

Be a good steward over your thoughts, your words, your heart. Be a good steward over your realm of influence over your household. We can't let our children run rampant; we have to teach them. We must be good stewards over all relationships in our lives, our marriages, our souls; watch what comes in and what goes out. Be confident in God, in your relationships, not in you. Working as unto God, not unto your own self. Bless the ones in Christ, pray for them.

Prayer: Lord, help us to find something productive to do as unto You. Help us not to waste time, money, the gifts and talents You have placed in us. God help us to do what You would have us to do, serve and not to be like anyone else. In Jesus' name. Amen.

Your Reflections

How Can You Apply This Message to Your Life?

_____
_____
_____
_____
_____
_____
_____
_____
_____
_____
_____
_____
_____
_____
_____
_____
_____
_____
_____
_____
_____
_____
_____
_____

Your Reflections

How Can You Apply This Message to Your Life?

_____

_____

_____

_____

_____

_____

_____

_____

_____

_____

_____

_____

_____

_____

_____

_____

_____

_____

_____

_____

_____

_____

_____

At the Table

Psalm 23

**You prepare a table before me in the presence of
my enemies;
You anoint my head with oil;
My cup runs over.
Surely goodness and mercy shall follow me
All the days of my life;
And I will dwell in the house of the Lord
Forever. (NKJV)**

Joy is here — the table is spread; the feast of the Lord
is going on. This is one of my favorite songs taken
from Psalm 23. Gentiles were invited in because the
Lord's people would not come, I have read several
accounts of the Israelites being invited and having
better or other things to do. Not having what they
needed, but they missed out when they had to go and
find it. I think God knew this would happen because
He wanted us and loved us so much.

We find joy in our sorrows, there's peace wherever
the table is spread. It is prepared for us right now.
Healing is at the table; financial security is at the
table whatever we need is there. Psalm 23:5 says God
will prepare a table for us in the presence of our

enemies, while the enemy plots and plans against us. God has what we need, out in the open in the presence of our enemies. In your workplace, when it doesn't look like you will be promoted, but you are given a position, God has a plan and a purpose for that: it's at the table.

In the presence of people who tried to hold you back. In the presence of people who do not value your contribution. You receive a reward, you may not have the perfect clothing, the right credentials or station in life, but the Bible says the wealth of the wicked is stored up for the righteous, there is plenty out there. At the table are dignitaries, people of importance, you didn't ask for it, didn't think you deserved it, was not expecting it. But when God gives you a place no one can take it away. If we seek first the kingdom of God, all these things will be added unto us. Your gift will make room for you.

Prayer: Lord, keep us steadfast in seeking You. Help us to obey You and continue growing in and knowing You. Help us to stop working in our own strength. Keep us out of Your way; Your way is better. Father, help us to help others and maintain our right standing with You. In Jesus' name. Amen.

Your Reflections

How Can You Apply This Message to Your Life?

_____

_____

_____

_____

_____

_____

_____

_____

_____

_____

_____

_____

_____

_____

_____

_____

_____

_____

_____

_____

_____

_____

_____

_____

Your Reflections

How Can You Apply This Message to Your Life?

_____

_____

_____

_____

_____

_____

_____

_____

_____

_____

_____

_____

_____

_____

_____

_____

_____

_____

_____

_____

_____

_____

_____

_____

Muscle Memory

Isaiah 35:3

Strengthen ye the weak hands, and confirm the feeble knees. (KJV)

Where there is damage in a home or damage in your body or disruption in your business, family, or your spiritual source, there is muscle memory. There are certain characteristics that teach it is time for a makeover, where there is rot and sagging, the house needs fortifying.

When houses have termite damage, you don't see it until you start digging in. Trying to make improvements, you see the evidence; you must find out what caused the damage. You don't have to disrupt the foundation; it's there. Call the Orkin man. Ask God to help you, to look at you, to fix it. With things eating at us slowly, we must do an overhaul — not just examine ourselves but ask God to look for any wicked way in us; fix it so we can continue.

Body issues. Ouch. You do not want to look at it or contemplate it. However, it is a must. Strokes causes damage and heart attacks disrupts your physical house, drugs and alcohol will shorten your life as well. God is our foundation, He is our deliverer, our healer and our restorer. He is our way of escape maker. We are fearfully and wonderfully made, and there is certain characteristic that causes muscle memory to come into play. The body wants to bounce back; with God all things are possible.

Fear of the unknown holds us back and keeps us from having confidence. With God we can strengthen our weak hands and feeble knees and pray.

Prayer: Thank You, Lord, that our minds can be stayed on You. That we recall Your word in times of need, that we don't have to fear trouble because You are stronger than our troubles. You want us to succeed and, most importantly, You want us to grow in our relationship with You. Thank You that fear has no place. You did not give us a spirit of fear but of power and of love and a sound mind. In Jesus' name. Amen.

Your Reflections

How Can You Apply This Message to Your Life?

_____

_____

_____

_____

_____

_____

_____

_____

_____

_____

_____

_____

_____

_____

_____

_____

_____

_____

_____

_____

_____

_____

_____

Your Reflections

How Can You Apply This Message to Your Life?

_____

_____
_____
_____
_____
_____
_____
_____
_____
_____
_____
_____
_____
_____
_____
_____
_____
_____
_____
_____
_____
_____
_____
_____
_____
_____

Employment to Deployment

John 16:7

But very truly I tell you, it is for your good that I am going away. Unless I go away, the Advocate will not come to you; but if I go, I will send him to you. (NIV)

The Word says to employ the Holy Spirit. He is the most important thing in your spiritual toolkit. Jesus sent Him to us when He went to sit on the right hand of His Father. He is on the inside of us and, whether we know it or not, He is here to keep us on the right course. He works on our behalf every day. Acknowledging Him and employing Him gives you the Word to say in the hour that you need them. Wisdom comes forth from that spiritual toolkit. Understanding and knowledge is made available.

A carpenter's toolkit has everything he needs. It must be used; the hammer and nails are readily recognized; some of the other tools still look new. Like these carpenters, our toolkit is well used in some areas: some of us pray daily, and kindness comes easy — you've been using them. As we access the precious spirit of God all our tools are employed the

Holy Spirit keeps us honed and growing, whether it be listening to God or loving a brother or sister.

The Holy Spirit is the most important tool to employ. When we have, we are versed in the fruit of the spirit, the beatitudes and the Word of God. When utilizing your other tools, before you know it, you have gone from employing the Holy Spirit to becoming fishers or recruiters of men. You have been deployed. You are now in the army of the Lord.

Prayer: Thank You, Lord, that we are now in Your army, marching onward to victory. Thank You that we have moved forward to show forth Your glory. Thank You that we understand the tools You have given us. Thank You for Your precious spirit for leading us and guiding us in every area of our lives. Thank You for a well-attended toolkit and the will to continue. In Jesus' name. Amen.

Your Reflections

How Can You Apply This Message to Your Life?

_____

_____

_____

_____

_____

_____

_____

_____

_____

_____

_____

_____

_____

_____

_____

_____

_____

_____

_____

_____

_____

_____

_____

_____

_____

Your Reflections

How Can You Apply This Message to Your Life?

_____

_____

_____

_____

_____

_____

_____

_____

_____

_____

_____

_____

_____

_____

_____

_____

_____

_____

_____

_____

_____

_____

Rare Pearls

Matthew 7:6

Give not that which is holy unto the dogs, neither cast ye your pearls before swine, lest they trample them under their feet, and turn again and rend you. (KJV)

It does not depend on who likes you. God has a plan and a purpose for your life. It is not dependent upon people who manipulate or have misplaced hostilities toward you. Jealousy comes into play; pay no attention to their faces. Be careful whom you share your feelings with, your thoughts, your dreams. Do not throw your pearls to swine. The pearls you have are rare. And be careful whom you allow access to. Some will turn and rend you. They don't understand how precious those pearls are, how rare they are. According to the world, Godly things are foolish.

Don't give away your gifts or let someone else have knowledge of and use against you. What God has given you is too precious to give someone else. Esau was the first born and privy to God's many favors and gifts. But he didn't value it. He was willing to sell what he had, jokingly, for a bowl of soup. Have you ever received something that you didn't appreciate until it was gone? A friendship, finances, a spouse? Don't take for granted what God has blessed you with.

If you want a friend, show yourself friendly, but be wise and don't bring the wrong person into your life. Learn to control whom you invest in, do not be an over sharer. They will turn and rend you. The precious things that God has given us need to be protected. They don't need to be bragged about; they don't need to be shown off. They need to be kept until the right time to use. Then those pearls of wisdom will come forth.

Prayer: Father God, thank You for the best things, the rarest things that You have only chosen for me. Thank You for molding me and shaping that I may be able to complete the task. Thank You for wisdom and understanding. In Jesus' name. Amen.

Your Reflections

How Can You Apply This Message to Your Life?

_____

_____

_____

_____

_____

_____

_____

_____

_____

_____

_____

_____

_____

_____

_____

_____

_____

_____

_____

_____

_____

_____

_____

_____

_____

_____

Your Reflections

How Can You Apply This Message to Your Life?

_____

_____

_____

_____

_____

_____

_____

_____

_____

_____

_____

_____

_____

_____

_____

_____

_____

_____

_____

_____

_____

_____

_____

_____

_____

What Ails You?

Galatians 5:7

You ran well. Who hindered you from obeying the truth?

When we find stress and strife in our lives, we are being trained for the next level. The next level is God and His plan for you. We have discussed our finances, our relationships, the things that so easily beset us. Things we are drawn to. We throw ourselves under the bus; we throw our pearls to swine.

Use wisdom in your conversations. Use discernment for relationships. Engage understanding be certain before getting into anything. Ask God for guidance. Is this person the right one for me? For your own well-being, remember who you used to be, what you used to do? Examine yourselves and make sure you are going in the right direction. Let go and let God order your steps.

Let us love one another as God has commended love toward us, that it might work in us, on us and through us in the name of Jesus. Don't let bitterness seep in, or jealousy build up. No one can take you from God's hand. We must suffer the consequences for our own choices, for leaning to our own understanding. We are what ails us. Ask God to use you to His glory, repent and continue.

Prayer: Father God, thank You for the wisdom that You have given me. I ask Your spirit to help me not to cast my pearls to swine and suffer dire consequences. Please help us to stay in our rightful places, grasp and hold on to faith, and trust in You. In Jesus' name. Amen.

Your Reflections

How Can You Apply This Message to Your Life?

_____
_____
_____
_____
_____
_____
_____
_____
_____
_____
_____
_____
_____
_____
_____
_____
_____
_____
_____
_____
_____
_____
_____
_____

Your Reflections

How Can You Apply This Message to Your Life?

_____

_____

_____

_____

_____

_____

_____

_____

_____

_____

_____

_____

_____

_____

_____

_____

_____

_____

_____

_____

_____

_____

_____

_____

_____

_____

Judgment

Luke 2:8–11

Now there were in the same country shepherds living out in the fields, keeping watch over their flock by night. And behold, an angel of the Lord stood before them, and the glory of the Lord shone around them, and they were greatly afraid. Then the angel said to them, "Do not be afraid, for behold, I bring you good tidings of great joy which will be to all people. For there is born to you this day in the city of David a Savior, who is Christ the Lord." (NKJV)

Jesus came and made salvation available for everyone: Muslims, Hindu, Jewish, Gentiles etc. — people who didn't accept Him. There were those who were excluded, but those who heard of His power would ask Him for help. People who would kill, lie, cheat and steal. Everyone was given the opportunity to receive Jesus Christ as their savior. We were all invited in.

Some will choose to be an enemy of the cross. However, with Christ, there is no more guilt, shame, or condemnation. Jesus came to save us. He gave us a choice and then lovingly told us: choose life. Not forcing, not demanding, but being obedient to our Father. The wealth of the wicked is stored up for the righteous. There are people out there giving and giving — seemingly kindhearted people but without Jesus it is in vain.

Forgiveness: there is no more guilt or condemnation. We must forgive ourselves, ask God for everything we need. Don't lean to our own understanding. If you have wronged someone; ask for forgiveness. God has graciously forgiven us. Jesus came to right the sin nature we inherited from Adam. You must receive, believe, trust in Christ, and all that He came to do will be added unto you.

Prayer: Thank You for Your awesome plan of redemption, for the opportunity to receive Your mercy, Your grace and goodness. I exalt You, lift You up and magnify Your Holy name. I sing praises to Your name and thank You for who You are. In Jesus' name. Amen.

Your Reflections

How Can You Apply This Message to Your Life?

_____

_____

_____

_____

_____

_____

_____

_____

_____

_____

_____

_____

_____

_____

_____

_____

_____

_____

_____

_____

_____

_____

Your Reflections

How Can You Apply This Message to Your Life?

_____
_____
_____
_____
_____
_____
_____
_____
_____
_____
_____
_____
_____
_____
_____
_____
_____
_____
_____
_____
_____
_____
_____
_____
_____

What Would We Do?

Mark 13:32–33

But of that day and hour no one knows, not even the angels in heaven, nor the Son, but only the Father. Take heed, watch and pray; for you do not know when the time is. (NKJV)

What would we do if we knew we only had a few days left on earth?

What regrets would we have?

What triumphs would we remember?

What victories would we share?

What things would seem so petty or insignificant?

Would we hold the ones we love closer?

Would we forgive them everything?

Would we love them as God has loved us?

Would we be selfish or selfless?

Would God's love for us come into play?

Would we even care?

Prayer: Thank You, Father, that You hear and answer prayers. Thank You that the answers we search for come from You. Thank You for the provisions You have given us. Help us to continue to lean on You and remember where our help comes from. We don't know what we would do without You. In Jesus' name. Amen.

Your Reflections

How Can You Apply This Message to Your Life?

_____
_____
_____
_____
_____
_____
_____
_____
_____
_____
_____
_____
_____
_____
_____
_____
_____
_____
_____
_____
_____
_____
_____
_____
_____
_____

Your Reflections

How Can You Apply This Message to Your Life?

_____
_____
_____
_____
_____
_____
_____
_____
_____
_____
_____
_____
_____
_____
_____
_____
_____
_____
_____
_____
_____
_____
_____
_____

What Is Your Motive?

Proverbs 16:2

**All the ways of a man are pure in his own eyes,
But the Lord weighs the spirits. (NKJV)**

Our motives determine whether God allows us to accomplish His goals for us. He will know if we are ready or not. Motives are reasons for doing something, especially things that are hidden or not obvious. Something that causes a person to act. Is it selfish or prideful, or is it to benefit the Kingdom of God? Are we thinking of ourselves, of finances, worldly goods, or are we praying, are we loving?

A story in the Bible that gives an account of a king who brings the spoils into the camp when they all were told not to. They went from great success to an epic failure; there was sin in the camp. Why did he do it? What was his motive? His whole family suffered the consequences of his actions. He did not put his trust in God. He did it for personal gain. Think about what we do for personal gain.

God is in the forgiving business, but the consequences for our actions can be hard to bear. We lose a lot when our motives are not pure. Sometimes we want to be blessed and make someone else feel bad. Our motives are wrong and do not give God the glory. We want money to make others jealous, when we should say, "if He did it for me, He will do it for you."

Prayer: Father, help us be exceptional examples of who You are in our lives. Let our motives be pure and acceptable in Your sight. Let the message from our mouths be blessings not curses, life and not death, light and not darkness. In Jesus' name. Amen.

Your Reflections

How Can You Apply This Message to Your Life?

_____

_____

_____

_____

_____

_____

_____

_____

_____

_____

_____

_____

_____

_____

_____

_____

_____

_____

_____

_____

_____

_____

_____

_____

Your Reflections

How Can You Apply This Message to Your Life?

_____
_____
_____
_____
_____
_____
_____
_____
_____
_____
_____
_____
_____
_____
_____
_____
_____
_____
_____
_____
_____
_____
_____
_____

Hiding Places

Matthew 5:14–16

"You are the light of the world. A city that is set on a hill cannot be hidden. Nor do they light a lamp and put it under a basket, but on a lampstand, and it gives light to all who are in the house. Let your light so shine before men, that they may see your good works and glorify your Father in heaven." (NKJV)

Most hiding places are in the dark. As children, we would hide in the closets, under the bed, the darkest places we could find, so we would not be found. We are quiet and still, barely breathing, to keep our secrets hidden. However, we would eventually be discovered. As adults, our intentions are the same when we deceive our bosses, our mates, our God. When David sent Bathsheba's husband to the front line to his death, he wanted to hide something. What are we hiding when we harbor impure deeds or thoughts, our own insecurity?

We have not put our whole heart in trusting God. Help us, Lord. What good is it to speak our mind — when we have the mind of Christ, we can rightly divide the Word of truth. We can cast down every vain imagination. We must find out what is important to God: compassion for others, encouraging one another. Share the Word of God with your family. God has a plan and a purpose for each of us. We don't have to worry about what someone else has. We must shine the light in the darkness and be the light so we can live our lives to the glory of God.

Prayer: Lord God, cleanse our hearts and minds. Help us to have the mind of Christ. And use what He has said to Your glory. Thank You, Father, for Your many blessings and that our motives are pure in Your sight. I thank You that we do not have to be concerned with what others think of us, however we must shine the light into the darkest places and please You. In Jesus' name. Amen.

Your Reflections

How Can You Apply This Message to Your Life?

_____

_____

_____

_____

_____

_____

_____

_____

_____

_____

_____

_____

_____

_____

_____

_____

_____

_____

_____

_____

_____

_____

_____

Your Reflections

How Can You Apply This Message to Your Life?

_____

_____

_____

_____

_____

_____

_____

_____

_____

_____

_____

_____

_____

_____

_____

_____

_____

_____

_____

_____

_____

_____

_____

_____

Write the Vision

Habakkuk 2:2–4

"Write the vision
And make it plain on tablets,
That he may run who reads it.
For the vision is yet for an appointed time;
But at the end it will speak, and it will not lie.
Though it tarries, wait for it;
Because it will surely come,
It will not tarry."
"Behold the proud,
His soul is not upright in him;
But the just shall live by his faith." (NKJV)

During one of the many times that Israel was going into captivity, God gave them the assurance that justice would be served. The nation that was used in God's judgment of His people would be subject to the same judgment. The promises God made about restoring His people talked about the covenant. You shall be My people, and I will be your God. This is not only material, political or natural, it was also a spiritual restoration of the covenant relationship between God and His people.

In the health ministry we restore health, we feed the poor, we take care of material needs, seek justice in a politically unjust environment. We uphold the ideas of God's word. His word is all good if we know or have been made aware of the core problem, which is a broken relationship with our creator. We will not know the vision; the purpose and plan God has for us if we don't know Him or discern His mission. God told Habakkuk to write it down so we could run with it.

We must see God's perspective. The big picture. Pray that He opens our eyes and lets us see His plan and purpose for our lives. God gave us potential, and He gave us all a plan and a purpose. We must write the vision, write it down, write our plans down, what we see, what we want to pray about, what we want to accomplish in life what the Word of God says according to those things.

The problems that the children of Israel had and the reason God pronounced judgment, was that the nation's troubles were described as sickness, wounds and bruises. So, their promise was for health. God knows all our problems, every part of our bodies, natural and spiritual issues. He promises that He would heal them of those wounds, pardon their sins, remove their afflictions and give them rest. We must allow Him to do it. We will be healed from captivity, of things of our own making and backsliding. We will have no more calamity as a promise. We must be confident in His deliverance in every area of our lives.

Prayer: Thank You, Lord, that the vision is written in Your word, and in our hearts that we may run and not get weary, walk and not faint. Thank You that the problems that people seek us out for in judgment, the same judgment will be applied to them as well. Help us to write Your vision with our lives and actions. Help us to keep You first. In Jesus' name. Amen.

Your Reflections

How Can You Apply This Message to Your Life?

_____

_____

_____

_____

_____

_____

_____

_____

_____

_____

_____

_____

_____

_____

_____

_____

_____

_____

_____

_____

_____

_____

_____

_____

Friends

Job 16:20-21

My intercessor is my friend[a] as my eyes pour out tears to God; on behalf of a man he pleads with God as one pleads for a friend. (NIV)

Friends call each other into the things of God. Friends make you remember what God has done for you. Friends call each other to faith, moments of laughter, moments of prayer, convictions and forgiveness. They call on the name of Jesus, for each other, they touch and agree together.

Jesus, Jesus, Jesus, the name above all names. Jesus the name above sickness and disease. His name cancels fear, anxiety and depression. Friends come together with authority in the name of Jesus. There is no doubt, no depression, insecurities or lack. Friends live in authority to put the enemy under their feet. Friends know that two are better than one.

Jesus is who you call on in the midnight hour, in the dark times. He is who we thank for hearing and answering prayers. Jesus is the way, the truth and the life. You cannot go to God without Him. If you want a friend, show yourself friendly. Jesus is the friend that is closer than a brother. Jesus, Jesus, Jesus, what a friend we have in Jesus.

Prayer: Thank You that we can call on Your name. Thank You that we are considered family members because we believe as You believe. Thank You for showing us how to be friendly, even laying down Your life for a friend, for us. Thank You. In Jesus' name. Amen.

Your Reflections

How Can You Apply This Message to Your Life?

_____
_____
_____
_____
_____
_____
_____
_____
_____
_____
_____
_____
_____
_____
_____
_____
_____
_____
_____
_____
_____
_____
_____
_____
_____
_____

Your Reflections

How Can You Apply This Message to Your Life?

_____
_____
_____
_____
_____
_____
_____
_____
_____
_____
_____
_____
_____
_____
_____
_____
_____
_____
_____
_____
_____
_____
_____
_____
_____

Change

Deuteronomy 2:3

**"You have skirted this mountain long enough;
turn northward." (NKJV)**

Once while walking and praying, talking to God, on
my regular route, I was impressed to go in another
direction. I did not want to go around this circle
again. So, I walked away from the playground and
went in a different direction. It was misting rain and
I met someone on the church step who wanted to
know why I was walking in the rain. It turns out that
they had a gym inside, a walking track that I could
use and I was invited in. I was thankful and went on
about my way.

The next time I went out, I visited the church and I
signed up to go in the gym. I began walking around
the track on the second floor. As I walked, of course,
I still prayed. I met someone who would be
instrumental to my next journey in ministry. I spent
the next year and a half doing the most rewarding
work; something heretofore, I could not have
imagined. Being in out of the rain was a bonus, too.

Once I changed direction, stopped going around the mountain, God sent my next assignment. He continuously has our plan in mind and a purpose for us. It may be time for a change if you find yourself going in circles. You know the Israelites went around the mountain for forty years before the promised land. Talk to God: He knows if you are ready and has it all mapped out for you.

Prayer: Thank You, Lord, for Your direction, not mine. Thank You that You are in time with my next steps and are ordering them. Thank You that Your way is better and already planned. Lead us all on our next journey and help us to act when You call us to go. Help us, Lord, to recognize when there is need for a change of mind and direction. In Jesus' name. Amen.

Your Reflections

How Can You Apply This Message to Your Life?

_____

_____

_____

_____

_____

_____

_____

_____

_____

_____

_____

_____

_____

_____

_____

_____

_____

_____

_____

_____

_____

_____

_____

_____

Your Reflections

How Can You Apply This Message to Your Life?

_____
_____
_____
_____
_____
_____
_____
_____
_____
_____
_____
_____
_____
_____
_____
_____
_____
_____
_____
_____
_____
_____

Superpowers

Judges 13:16

And the Angel of the Lord said to Manoah, "Though you detain Me, I will not eat your food. But if you offer a burnt offering, you must offer it to the Lord." (For Manoah did not know He was the Angel of the Lord.) (NKJV)

From the account in the Bible, Samson had superhuman strength. His body was strong and he won plenty of battles. He even killed thousands of Philistines with the jawbone of an ass. Quite impressive; however, he had a weakness for pretty women. He allowed a woman to take him in, to cut his long, beautiful hair. He lost the power to slay the enemy and lost his freedom. He had the physical strength to accomplish his mission but was not mindful of his instruction and lost it all.

Solomon was wise, had superhuman wisdom. Wiser than any man or woman of his time. It was God-given wisdom that he asked for himself. Like Samson, he did not obey God and began to worship other gods, accumulated other idols and his superpower was lost. There are very many accounts in the Bible that let us witness the consequences of losing your superpowers, which is the anointing of God.

Once you lose focus and are swayed from God's original intention, then you are no longer operating in His plan. The children of Israel's lives became more difficult, strength and wisdom were superseded by their disobedience. There are many of us that have superpowers, the anointing; if we ignore it, don't appreciate it or value it, we must work harder to get the job done. It is more profitable when God works.

Wherever we are, wherever we go, God is with us and will accomplish in us what He planned. The world is consumed with superheroes, good versus evil, all shapes and sizes, cartoons, anime, and man sculpted into muscle suits. All we need is God's plan for our lives and the faith to carry it through. It's real: God's supernatural chosen and protected with favor, someone qualified, with the authority to act with His approval.

Prayer: God, thank you that we do not need superhuman power as the world offers. All we need is your supernatural power. The anointing of God. Awesome. In Jesus' name. Amen.

Your Reflections

How Can You Apply This Message to Your Life?

_____

_____

_____

_____

_____

_____

_____

_____

_____

_____

_____

_____

_____

_____

_____

_____

_____

_____

_____

_____

_____

_____

_____

_____

Your Reflections

How Can You Apply This Message to Your Life?

_____

_____

_____

_____

_____

_____

_____

_____

_____

_____

_____

_____

_____

_____

_____

_____

_____

_____

_____

_____

_____

_____

_____

_____

Say it Loud!

Psalm 150:1

Praise the Lord!
Praise God in His sanctuary;
Praise Him in His mighty firmament! (NKJV)

I have found that reading the Word out loud, praying the Word audibly as well fulfills a requirement of God's word. Confessing and professing the Word is necessary when getting the Word on the inside. Faith comes by hearing and hearing by the Word of God. It does not matter who is speaking. Why not you?

You sow a seed into the kingdom when your words of confidence are planted into your heart. God has given us a mustard seed of faith. You could say, "so say it loud, who better than you?" In the sanctuary, praise His goodness, testify of His love, grace, and mercy. He does not need our praise and worship; He can make the rocks cry out if we do not. It is not for Him but for us. We benefit from saying it loud, acknowledging His presence in our lives, observing His wonderous work, in heaven and earth, in us.

Establishing a relationship with our Father in Heaven, singing psalms and hymns goes to the core of our individual existence, the most beneficial gift that we can give and receive, so SAY IT LOUD! Start today, in your prayer room, in the kitchen or the bathroom. Once we understand the benefit of blessing the Lord in this manner, you will have one more tool in your tool belt to implement change in your life.

Prayer: Thank You, Father, for Your many blessings, for Your consideration for us in all things. Thank You for the faith and confidence we have in You. Help us, Lord, to be an example to others and make a positive change in our special relationship with You. In Jesus' name. Amen.

Your Reflections

How Can You Apply This Message to Your Life?

_____

_____

_____

_____

_____

_____

_____

_____

_____

_____

_____

_____

_____

_____

_____

_____

_____

_____

_____

_____

_____

_____

_____

_____

_____

Your Reflections

How Can You Apply This Message to Your Life?

_____

_____

_____

_____

_____

_____

_____

_____

_____

_____

_____

_____

_____

_____

_____

_____

_____

_____

_____

_____

_____

_____

_____

_____

Practice Prayer

Matthew 6:9–13

After this manner therefore pray ye: Our Father which art in heaven, Hallowed be thy name.
Thy kingdom come, Thy will be done in earth, as it is in heaven.
Give us this day our daily bread.
And forgive us our debts, as we forgive our debtors.
And lead us not into temptation, but deliver us from evil: For thine is the kingdom, and the power, and the glory, forever. Amen. (KJV)

The Lord's Prayer is a prayer given by Jesus to His disciples when they asked Him to teach them to pray. We call it the model prayer, and many denominations say the prayer as it is. Some use it as a guideline to pray. Whichever you choose, you cannot go wrong. This prayer covers what you need to communicate efficiently with God.

So, we pray to the Father, in the name of Jesus, by the precious Spirit of God. We make our request known to God. We tell Him what we have need of. Is there anything that you are believing God for, praying for or waiting for? Figure out what you need to pray for. It can be a necessity or a desire of your heart. Prayer is paramount in building your relationship with God.

Now pray for it. Ask God for it. Pray according to His will. Do not pray amiss, praying for thing that are not yours. Pray according to His will and for the ability to believe that you will receive what you ask for. When you pray, if He hears your prayer, if your prayer is in faith and authentic you will have the desires of your heart. You can go boldly to the throne of grace and ask for the big things. Go for it.

Meditate on the Word repeatedly, ask for understanding. Have a brother or sister to agree in prayer with you. Thank God for hearing and answering prayers. Lastly, remind Him of what you asked for, believe and wait.

Prayer: Thank You, Lord, for Your instruction that has been written. Thank You, Father, for Your Son, Jesus Christ, making it possible for everyone's salvation and the ability to come boldly before You with confidence. Thank You for waiting for us. In Jesus' name. Amen.

Your Reflections

How Can You Apply This Message to Your Life?

_____

_____

_____

_____

_____

_____

_____

_____

_____

_____

_____

_____

_____

_____

_____

_____

_____

_____

_____

_____

_____

_____

_____

_____

_____

Your Reflections

How Can You Apply This Message to Your Life?

_____
_____
_____
_____
_____
_____
_____
_____
_____
_____
_____
_____
_____
_____
_____
_____
_____
_____
_____
_____
_____
_____
_____
_____

Reclaim Your Day

Colossians 3:12

Therefore, as God's chosen people, holy and dearly loved, clothe yourselves with compassion, kindness, humility, gentleness and patience. (NIV)

My oldest grandson went through a phase of disobedience, having meltdowns, total rebellion against his parents and teachers. No one knew how to control him; he had always been mild mannered and quiet. However, here he was at the age of 5 becoming a menace. They tried everything from time out to withholding things. He continued to get worse and did not respond to rewards, either.

He was a sweet kid with dimples and big puppy dog eyes. The sudden change in his behavior had everyone baffled. His teacher continued to have patience with him and reminded him often that there was still time for him to reclaim his day. The family soon adopted this tactic, and he slowly began to reclaim his day. I thank God for his teacher's patience and continual, unconditional support of him.

God is like that with us: He loves us, and He waits for us to get up time and time again. Repeatably, He forgives, reaches out a hand to help us. While we are trying to do things our way, work to make things happen in our strength. We have access to His love, peace and joy. When we have taken the wrong turn and the way is not so straight and narrow any more, He is there. Saul had an encounter with God and was able to become Paul.

Prayer: Thank You, Lord, for telling us that we still have time to reclaim our day. In Jesus' name. Amen.

Your Reflections

How Can You Apply This Message to Your Life?

_____
_____
_____
_____
_____
_____
_____
_____
_____
_____
_____
_____
_____
_____
_____
_____
_____
_____
_____
_____
_____
_____
_____
_____

Your Reflections

How Can You Apply This Message to Your Life?

_____
_____
_____
_____
_____
_____
_____
_____
_____
_____
_____
_____
_____
_____
_____
_____
_____
_____
_____
_____
_____
_____
_____

Identity Crisis

John 1:12

But as many as received Him, to them He gave the right to become children of God, to those who believe in His name. (NKJV)

We as the children of God, constantly go through ups and downs, great highs and lows. Things change in a heartbeat, just when we think we are OK. It's hard. The wind comes, and the rain comes. Sometimes we are in sinking sand, being tossed to and from with every wind and doctrine. Sickness, finances, children, grandchildren and your ministry. This sounds like a major identity crisis.

We, the children of God, have forgotten our station in life. We have forgotten whose we are and who we are. We are the head and not the tail, above only not beneath. We are a part of a royal priesthood. An ambassador to Christ. We are saved, sanctified and set apart unto God. Heir with the Son, co-heir with the Father. We can do all things through Christ who strengthens us.

We have inherited all the promises and things that were accomplished while Jesus was here and those taken on the cross with Him. Yet, we still fear the problems we encounter along with the light afflictions that come. We forget who we are and who is interceding for us. Jesus died and left grace to account for all our sins, there is no more guilt or condemnation, no shame. What do we have to fear when we once again have been set up for success? It was in the plan all along. It is not how we feel, the circumstances encountered but the foundation Christ laid for us.

Prayer: Thank You, Father, that we were made in Your image and likeness, giving us a sure identity, a sure foundation on the rock. Thank You for Your consistent care and concern for Your children. Thanks for the power to become sons of God. Help us hold fast to our confession of faith. In Jesus' name. Amen.

Your Reflections

How Can You Apply This Message to Your Life?

_____

_____

_____

_____

_____

_____

_____

_____

_____

_____

_____

_____

_____

_____

_____

_____

_____

_____

_____

_____

_____

_____

_____

Your Reflections

How Can You Apply This Message to Your Life?

_____

_____

_____

_____

_____

_____

_____

_____

_____

_____

_____

_____

_____

_____

_____

_____

_____

_____

_____

_____

_____

_____

_____

_____

_____

_____

SOS

Psalm 6:3–4

My soul also is greatly troubled;
But You, O Lord—how long?

Return, O Lord, deliver me!
Oh, save me for Your mercies' sake!

"SOS" has been used by the Navy and personal vessels that have encountered trouble for many years. When ships were sinking or when stranded, SOS would be used as a cry for help (because it was an easy combination of letters in Morse code). It let someone know about the distress you were in, that you had somehow lost your way by accident or no fault of your own. It came to mean "Save Our Souls" in the natural, as well as in the spiritual sense. SOS was used in a way that was meant to get you out of harm's way.

When we call out to God because we have lost our way, that trouble has come upon us, we can be certain, as ship captains were, that help would be sent. You do not have to be ashamed when you need help from God, just call on Him and you will be saved.

When we are in trouble, we are too proud to tell someone, but people see the wreckage in your life. They see the change in you, the change in your behavior. When the enemy is influencing you, making you think you are always right, blaming, accusing, condemning and judging other people because you cannot get it together. King David was awesome in his approach to God for help. He asked God who would praise Him if He put him in the pit. Be a man/woman after God's heart.

Prayer: Thank You, Lord, for giving us a way of escape, that we can come to You in times of trouble. The world's way is to say, "Stuck on Stupid." The Word's way is to ask God to Save our Souls. In Jesus' name. Amen.

Your Reflections

How Can You Apply This Message to Your Life?

_____
_____
_____
_____
_____
_____
_____
_____
_____
_____
_____
_____
_____
_____
_____
_____
_____
_____
_____
_____
_____
_____
_____
_____
_____

Your Reflections

How Can You Apply This Message to Your Life?

_____
_____
_____
_____
_____
_____
_____
_____
_____
_____
_____
_____
_____
_____
_____
_____
_____
_____
_____
_____
_____
_____
_____

Before You Speak — Think

Ephesians 4:27

"Be angry, and do not sin": do not let the sun go down on your wrath, nor give place to the devil. (NKJV)

Do not allow seeds to be planted that give place to the enemy. Whether we speak negative or positive words about ourselves or others. Seeds are planted and the words we say or receive can take root:

T — Is it True? John 1:14–16. Is it from God or is it the world?

H — Is it Helpful? What we say can be harmful. We ask the Holy Spirit to give us the words we need in the hour that we need them.

I — Is it Inspiring? Leaders are to inspire; the disciples inspired followers by speaking to others what Jesus had spoken to them.

N — Is it Necessary? The words we speak or share with someone may be true. We must discern when to say it and who to say it to. We do not have to always be right. Hold your peace until the right time.

K — Is it Kind? If we cannot think of anything nice to say, do not say anything. Kindness is one of the Fruits of the Spirit. The rest are in 2 Peter 1:7.

The Word says that even a fool seems wise if he does not speak.

Prayer: Thank You, Father, that we have the mind of Christ, rightly dividing the Word of truth. Thank You for Your knowledge, wisdom and understanding. Thank You that we are not ignorant of the devices of the enemy. Help us to continue to think before we speak. In Jesus' name. Amen.

Your Reflections

How Can You Apply This Message to Your Life?

_____

_____

_____

_____

_____

_____

_____

_____

_____

_____

_____

_____

_____

_____

_____

_____

_____

_____

_____

_____

_____

_____

_____

Your Reflections

How Can You Apply This Message to Your Life?

_____

_____

_____

_____

_____

_____

_____

_____

_____

_____

_____

_____

_____

_____

_____

_____

_____

_____

_____

_____

_____

_____

_____

_____

Be Thankful

Proverbs 16:18

Pride goes before destruction, And a haughty spirit before a fall. (NKJV)

Things that God hates:

A proud look: eyes looking down on others, thinking oneself is better than others. Expecting people to move out of your way. In essence saying, look what I have, I am part of the right family, and so forth.

Haughtiness: the whole way you carry yourself. Criticizing servers at restaurants, not tipping, making a scene. We should be thankful, putting others first. Thanking people for serving us from the greatest to the smallest, staying God's example no matter what. The fall is great.

A lying tongue: our tongue is a small thing that can do great damage. It can ruin someone's relationship or reputation. When you go as the world does to "spill the tea," this can set your own soul on fire, and you set a snare for yourself. Ouch, life and death is in the power of the tongue.

Feet swift to run to mischief: Running from house to house, not listening to the Spirit of God. Having to be in the thick of things. It is premeditated, planned ahead of time.

False witness: lying, killing me softly with your tongue.

Sowing discard among the brethren: Do we have to say any more? Causing trouble in the church. Unity is our goal; look and see where there is room for improvement individually in our own life so that we can all be on one accord. These things are deadly to our witness, to our credibility, ministry; we all have one.

Prayer: Thank You, Lord, for spelling it out. We know without a shadow of doubt what You expect from us. Thank You that You hate these things, because You know how much harm they will cause us as Your children. Thank You for making it plain. In Jesus' name. Amen.

Your Reflections

How Can You Apply This Message to Your Life?

_____
_____
_____
_____
_____
_____
_____
_____
_____
_____
_____
_____
_____
_____
_____
_____
_____
_____
_____
_____
_____
_____
_____
_____

Your Reflections

How Can You Apply This Message to Your Life?

_____
_____
_____
_____
_____
_____
_____
_____
_____
_____
_____
_____
_____
_____
_____
_____
_____
_____
_____
_____
_____
_____
_____
_____
_____

FOMO

Genesis 37:3

Now Israel loved Joseph more than all his children, because he was the son of his old age. Also he made him a tunic of many colors. (NKJV)

Joseph was the favorite son of his father; he also had a coat of many colors, made by his father. This made his 12 brothers, not just unhappy but extremely jealous. So, when he came out to tell them about his dream, that was the last straw. He had a major dream, and he informed his brothers that he would rule over them, that they would be subject to him. The brothers were struck with a bad case of FOMO: Fear of Missing Out. It is a worldly term, used in today's vernacular, but it even applied back in Joseph's time as well. The brothers could only see what they were missing. They were beside themselves; not only was he the favorite, but everyone knew it. They saw the way their father coddled him and how much he thought of himself.

The brothers schemed about what to do with him; instead of killing him, they deceived their father with animal blood on his coat, put him in a deep hole and later sold him to the Egyptians. Very extreme behavior especially for brothers, but the fear of missing out is very powerful. Lacking parental love, financials, better clothes, better jobs: anything that you think you might miss out on. It seems unfair for a coworker to get a promotion or to make more money. Your neighbor has a new car and yours is 10 years old.

When we go down the path of jealousy, envy, covetousness, we lay a trap for ourselves. They lead to a path of unrighteousness, and we snare ourselves. You have probably heard the rest of the story about Joseph, how he eventually became second in charge to Pharoah. He saved his family during famine and forgave them their crime against him. God has a plan and a purpose for all of us, good and not evil plans.

While FOMO is real, and things seem a certain way, make the right choice and believe that God has something just as special for you. Don't covet things that others have; cast your cares on Jesus because he cares for us. In the end, even though Joseph had a great position, Joseph ended up serving them. He had food for them and a place for them to live in the land of Goshen, until the famine was over. He had power and authority to get them anything they needed. See, there was no need for the brothers to have worried about missing out at all.

Prayer: Thank You, Father, that we do not have to fear anything, that as we seek You and trust You, all our desires, needs and wants will be met. Thank You that all things are working together for good, for us as well. In Jesus' name. Amen.

Your Reflections

How Can You Apply This Message to Your Life?

_____

_____

_____

_____

_____

_____

_____

_____

_____

_____

_____

_____

_____

_____

_____

_____

_____

_____

_____

_____

_____

_____

_____

_____

Reverent Demands

2 Timothy 2:15

Study to shew thyself approved unto God, a workman that needeth not to be ashamed, rightly dividing the word of truth. (KJV)

2 Timothy says, "Study to show thyself approve unto God, a workman that need not to be ashamed, rightly dividing the Word of truth." God comes and searches to find someone who is ready and willing.

He cannot choose us for the job if we do not know the material, if we have not tried God at His word. Something as simple as paying our tithes and offerings can deem us faithful and place us in the position to present a (reverent) demand on God's Word. In the Old Testament, "Bring ye all the tithes into the storehouse, that there may be meat in mine house, and prove me now herewith, saith the Lord of hosts, if I will not open you the windows of heaven, and pour you out a blessing, that there shall not be room enough to receive it. And I will rebuke the devourer for your sakes…." (Malachi 3:10–11 KJV). He says He would rebuke the devourer, which could be in our finances, in our relationships, in our ministries and at our workplaces — the things that come to try our faith and make us waiver where the promises of God are concerned. We must take God at His word and have faith that what He says is true. We literally must pray, "Father God, I pay my tithes and I need You to help me where my finances are concerned," or "God, my marriage is not working out, I pay my tithes and I need You to rebuke the devourer in our lives. Lord, I need You to open up that window." We are not paying God but obeying Him. God said it, He will do it. In the New Testament we are told that we can purpose in our own heart what we will give if we give cheerfully. It is the grace of God that gives us this option. Awesome. That choice can be what Abraham did or your own choice, net or gross does not matter to God. It is your heart that He is concerned with.

Our Father has a vested interest in us. He created us for Himself, and He is faithful to His word. He says, "For I know the thoughts that I think toward you, saith the Lord, thoughts of peace, and not evil, to give you an expected end." (Jeremiah 29:11 KJV). Believe it or not, God wants us more than the enemy, we are God's children, and He supersedes all else.

Prayer: Thank You, Lord, that Your life is not a fairy tale or seem improbable to us. Thank You, Lord, that You are looking and waiting for us to be prepared. In Jesus' name. Amen.

Your Reflections

How Can You Apply This Message to Your Life?

_____
_____
_____
_____
_____
_____
_____
_____
_____
_____
_____
_____
_____
_____
_____
_____
_____
_____
_____
_____
_____
_____
_____

Your Reflections

How Can You Apply This Message to Your Life?

_____

_____

_____

_____

_____

_____

_____

_____

_____

_____

_____

_____

_____

_____

_____

_____

_____

_____

_____

_____

_____

_____

_____

_____

_____

"Think on These Things"

Philippians 4:8

Finally, brethren, whatsoever things are true, whatsoever things are honest, whatsoever things are just, whatsoever things are pure, whatsoever things are lovely, whatsoever things are of good report; if there be any virtue, and if there be any praise, think on these things. (KJV) In other words, Godly Things.

How to think on these things: Isaiah 26:3 He will keep him in perfect peace whose mind is stayed on Him.

Renew your mind it is part of our soul, its prosperity is contingent upon what we think, our mind, will, emotions, our choices and how we feel.

Cast down all vain imaginations every high thing that exalts itself above the throne of God and make it line up with the Word of Jesus Christ.

As a man thinks: We have been thinking the wrong way for a long time, if we think the wrong way and not renew our mind and our focus (someone owes me something), is always someone else's fault and not our own.

Yes, there were numerous injustices done to us, but we have fought with the wrong weapons. We are part of God's kingdom. As we think on these things, we need to fight spiritual battle with spiritual weapons.

I put before you, life and death, blessings not curses. We must choose to think on God's things.

My hometown has great potential; that's good news. It has been there forever, still there and has a future, when we correct what we think. The evil report is not from God, but from what we think and speak.

Ms. Matthews — 6th grade English, taught me to defend myself.

Mr. Anderson — 8th grade SS class challenged me and pushed me.

In Mr. McBride's Black History class, I learned to improvise and that I liked to get up in front of class and give an oral book report.

Ms. Long gave me a love of words.

In my 1st grade class at my table, I learned leadership.

My hometown has many things to offer. We must think on these things and make our choice and choose life.

Prayer: Thank You, Lord, that as things seem to look bad, You give us the words to say that are good and positive. As we learn how to speak a good outcome into a negative situation, we see God operating on our behalf. Thank You that my hometown has the potential to thrive, no matter how it looks. In Jesus' name. Amen.

Your Reflections

How Can You Apply This Message to Your Life?

_____

_____

_____

_____

_____

_____

_____

_____

_____

_____

_____

_____

_____

_____

_____

_____

_____

_____

_____

_____

_____

_____

_____

_____

_____

It Takes a Village

1 Corinthians 4:14

I do not write these things to shame you, but as my beloved children I warn you. (NKJV)

To raise a child in the admonition of the Lord imposes God's way and understanding the importance of His will. Spending quality time with them, praying with them and taking them to church, proves to be an important component in raising a child. Manners and good behavior are an added advantage of God's way.

Many of us have experienced negative occurrences while attending church. I have heard many instances from former church-goers from thinking the pastor is misappropriating funds to people not speaking or thinking they are not good enough. For anyone interested, I believe that God's way is the best and only way. While we are in the world, God's grace is sufficient, He is continually leading us to His plan and purpose.

His will for us has been planned from the very beginning. So, every experience, situation, issue or circumstance is used to get us to our ultimate destination, the knowledge of Christ and His eternal plans. The enemy or the adversary, the devil has a plan for us and wants us to follow him. With our own free will and the enemy roaming around, we need our instruction manual more than ever. God has entrusted us to train His children and use whatever available to turn the children into mighty men and women of God.

Psychologists and all the research are ever changing. Debates over probabilities and possibilities are ongoing. God's Word never changes. He is the same forever and His love and care for us is everlasting. Training our children and making sure that they have a winning hand is the parents' responsibility. With the help of the church and government and doctors, their extended family, and friends, live by the Word of God.

Prayer: Thank You, Lord, for the villagers, the kindhearted, the teachers, doctors, for moms and dads, grammas, and grandpas. Thank You for the Bible that houses the truth, that when they are old, they will not forget. Thank You for entrusting them with us. In the name of Jesus. Amen.

Your Reflections

How Can You Apply This Message to Your Life?

_____

_____

_____

_____

_____

_____

_____

_____

_____

_____

_____

_____

_____

_____

_____

_____

_____

_____

_____

_____

_____

_____

_____

_____

_____

Your Reflections

How Can You Apply This Message to Your Life?

_____
_____
_____
_____
_____
_____
_____
_____
_____
_____
_____
_____
_____
_____
_____
_____
_____
_____
_____
_____
_____
_____

Contrast

2 Corinthians 5:17

Therefore, if anyone is in Christ, he is a new creation; old things have passed away; behold, all things have become new. (NKJV)

The difference or contrast that you see in a person, music or movie in the end or over time, can be polar opposite of where it began. Music or singing intensifies throughout a song and can change to convey a different thought or attitude. The music is beautiful and soft then changes to present other emotions. The contrast is what makes the song or music interesting and engaging.

When we see a change in people, the old man goes from old ways and becomes the new creation, leaving an inconvenient lifestyle to accepting Jesus as his Savior and choosing a life that is acceptable to God. Believing in his heart and confessing with his mouth that Jesus is the Son of God. The contrast should be so obvious that your friends think you have joined a cult, or they just do not understand the change, the difference they see.

We see the moon in a dark sky and the contrast is visible to the naked eye; with God's children, the change is happening from the inside out. The change is gradual, sometimes bumpy or difficult; nevertheless, the evidence slowly become obvious. The black ink on this white page helps me to see, to read and to witness the words that are on it. It helps me see the transformation as thoughts and ideas come forth.

Prayer: Thank You, Lord, for the changes You have made in me. Thank You for the way I think, act, and see myself. The contrast that has occurred in me has been a blessing. What was once on the inside is evident on the outside. Because of how You have worked in my life, I can see my children's future. Thank You that all the praise, glory and the honor go to You. In Jesus' name. Amen.

Your Reflections

How Can You Apply This Message to Your Life?

_____

_____

_____

_____

_____

_____

_____

_____

_____

_____

_____

_____

_____

_____

_____

_____

_____

_____

_____

_____

_____

_____

_____

_____

_____

Your Reflections

How Can You Apply This Message to Your Life?

_____

_____

_____

_____

_____

_____

_____

_____

_____

_____

_____

_____

_____

_____

_____

_____

_____

_____

_____

_____

_____

_____

_____

Courageous

Deuteronomy 31:6-7

"Be strong and courageous. Do not be afraid or terrified because of them, for the Lord your God goes with you; he will never leave you nor forsake you. Then Moses summoned Joshua and said to him in the presence of all Israel, "Be strong and courageous, for you must go with this people into the land that the Lord swore to their ancestors to give them, and you must divide it among them as their inheritance." (NIV)

In the movie "The Wizard of Oz," there is a cowardly lion; however, by nature a lion is one of the bravest and courageous animals in the jungle. He felt safe when he joined his friends. He was operating in opposition to his natural call. Moses was a man called of God; he made some serious mistakes, yet God still commissioned him to go when the time was right.

Moses did not embrace the anointing God had placed on him to get the job done. He had to take his brother, Aaron with him because of his lack of courage. Abraham did the same with Lot. God called Gideon a mighty man of valor. He was afraid and would not go without Deborah, who was a judge during the book of Judges.

There were different consequences for each of them, yet God used them with all their frailties, fear, and faults. They accomplished their goals and made a name for themselves in the Bible. Now it comes to us, called of God, we know the stories, we have seen the outcome and yet we are still not saved, the summer is spent. We fear what people think, what they say, who they are, when God has called and equipped us to go forth. We want to be like the world, be like the girls, hang with the boys, so we do not miss out.

With His will and His way, if He be for us, who can be against us. We have prayed and gone bravely to the throne of grace. We have desires of our heart that God has promised, yet we want someone to take with us. Watch out for haters and naysayers, family, and frenemies. Stay humble as we walk this walk; it is always nice to have someone to share your visions with, but not always profitable. Some people are not ready to go and cannot handle your success.

Prayer: Thank You, Lord, for life's lessons and Your wisdom. Thank You for examples in Your Word to learn from. I pray for each of our missions to be successful and accomplish what You have intended. Your will be done, not mine. In Jesus' name. Amen.

Your Reflections

How Can You Apply This Message to Your Life?

_____
_____
_____
_____
_____
_____
_____
_____
_____
_____
_____
_____
_____
_____
_____
_____
_____
_____
_____
_____
_____
_____
_____
_____
_____
_____

Your Reflections

How Can You Apply This Message to Your Life?

_____
_____
_____
_____
_____
_____
_____
_____
_____
_____
_____
_____
_____
_____
_____
_____
_____
_____
_____
_____
_____
_____
_____
_____
_____
_____

9 781959 543060